CHAPTER I - THE TIME OF THE EVENING SACRIFICE

Rolma sprinted through the large gate of her ancestral home and stopped for a moment to take in her surroundings. A small wooden water bucket was placed on her right hip and positioned on her back. The bucket was secured by a rope that was tied around her chest and the pail. The load was light at the moment because the pail was empty. It was empty, except for a wooden dipper that had been thrown into it. This was her last trip in the day, as the sun was setting at the rim of the surrounding mountains. Already, the foothills of the lower tier were covered in purple mists and the tall fields of wheat took on the dark shapes of twilight.

Before breakfast, her first water load was carried. It had looked easy with the warm sun and singing birds. One stray yak wandered along the path and she swiftly threw a clod full of earth at it. The yak had run so fast that it had fallen off the path, and she laughed with all her heartiness over the eleven years.

She didn't laugh because it was dark soon, which was something she feared. It was so quiet tonight that it was almost frightening. It seemed like there was fear in the air. As a chilling evening breeze suddenly swept across the fields in front her house, she felt a slight chill. She pulled her dark blue dress tighter around her and ran down the narrow track to the spring located at the foot the sacred tree.

Many prayer flags made of paper floated in the wind, despite being hung on the tree by religious believers. Drolma was nervous about them tonight, so she ran to get the water in her bucket. After filling the bucket, she moved swiftly to her hip and swung the water on to her hip. She bent forward under the weight and pulled on the rope in front. With a slow, steady swinging step she followed the track to her homestead, puffing slightly beneath the burden of her burden. The fine plaits on her head swung against her back, making

rhythmic jingles at each step. These coins were worn by all the village's unmarried daughters so their mothers could hear them and know they weren't causing mischief.

One stray yak wandering in the mountains

A cluster of mud homes made up the village where Drolma lived was all that remained. These houses were inhabited by settled Tibetans and a few Chinese or Mongols who had intermarried. Nomad Tibetans lived in tents made of yak hair and secluded in the grasslands. The monastery was located on the hillside above the village with its chanting hall and idol house, as well as many other dwellings for the priests. The towering chorten[2] and white-washed walls were stunning when the sun shined on them. Drolma has gazed at it since her childhood, sometimes in reverence, and sometimes in fear.

Drolma lived in a small village made up of a few mud houses. The monastary was located on the hill above the village.

Her mother would take her to the monastery on special occasions, where they dressed up in their finest and presented their votive offerings to the shrines. Drolma enjoyed the fun of these outings with her girl friends. They laughed and had fun in the sun. She was terrified to enter the darkened halls and grasped her mother's hands tightly. The god of hell was her special horror. One glance at it almost paralyzed her. The monotonous drumming and blowing of conch shells and horns, as priests chanted for long periods, made her head numb. These priests sat cross-legged on their small dais, and had a deep, chanting voice that seemed to be coming from the depths of their souls. After she had looked inside the dimly lit, gaily decorated chanting hall and noticed a few priests staring at her, she fled immediately.

Drolma's family could have been very wealthy if they hadn't had to pay so much tax to the monastery. Each year, the best of their wheat or barley was measured into long, narrow bags that were then hung on the backs for transport to the monastery's granary.

One monk in the monastery was generous, rather than grasping, and a giver as much as a recipient. He was referred to by the villagers in quiet tones as "The Precious one." He gave them seed-grain to plant their fields during a famine year. Drolma, a young child, had lost her father when he was just a few years old. His'reincarnation" was much younger than Drolma.

These thoughts were present in her mind when she reached her father's gateway and carried water to the other side of the courtyard. She then emptied the water into an earthenware container and turned it upside down so that it would drain until morning. She then took off her felt peaked hat and hung the bucket on a wooden peg against the mud wall. From the kitchen, her mother called.

"Daughter, close your front gate!" It's getting dark." Drolma returned to the front gate to close the double doors that separated them from the outside. As she was closing the second door, Drolma heard the faint tinkle from the small monastery bell.

She stepped outside and looked intently at the sound. She recognized the person ringing the bell. Her second brother was an acolyte at the monastery. He was sixteen years old and had been devoted to the priesthood since his birth. He was a great admirer of her, but his arrogant ways made her mad and sad.

Dorlma's second-brother was dedicated to the priesthood since his birth.

Sh e knew the reason he was ringing his bell at dusk. It was the hour of the evening sacrifice. Already, her brother would have placed several bowls full of wheat flour in the various openings of the small stone shrine. He lit the fire under each one, then he began to smoke. As the smoke rose into the still air, and the scent of burning grain filled the yard with its aroma, he was ringing a bell to summon the spirits and to call them to the altar to receive the costly offering. He would never neglect this offering lest a terrible retribution befall the monastery!

CHAPTER II - THE PRECIOUS ONE

Drolma, hen Drolma entered the house, found her mother cooking bread in boiling vegetable oil to prepare for the evening meal. A large, copper-plated teapot filled with boiling milky tea was sitting beside the fire. The father was now lying on the large mud bed, having taken off his leather boots. The kang (or bed) was heated by the same fire and connected to the stove via flues. He was talking to his youngest son, who would soon turn twenty-years old. They were discussing irrigation of their fields. Drolma was so familiar with these conversations that she didn't pay much attention to them tonight.

However, she slipped off her boots and walked across the room nakedfoot to help her younger brother's wife make tea. Soon, the five residents of the home were enjoying tea and bread. The men sat at the small table on the kang and the women sat on the floor or along the edges of the bed.

Drolma quickly finished her task and sat down on the ground, leaning against a wall, while the adults reminisced about the day. This harmless conversation is common in small villages all over the globe. Drolma noticed that incense sticks had been lit by her sister-in law and were placed in front of the small, enshrined Buddha Maitreya (the Buddha toCome) in the corner. Her eyes scanned the silk scarf in pale blue hanging on the wall. Drolma was looking at it as her mother lit the tiny vegetable oil lamp. As the lamp shrank, a flash of light sparked the silk scarf with splendor at the exact moment Drolma was looking at it. The scarf was the most treasured possession in the house, and Drolma's face lit up as she looked at it. The Precious One presented the scarf to her parents in return for the appropriate gifts her second brother brought into the monastery. It was a token to his blessing and

they were so grateful to have it. Drolma had received the scarf just before her birth. She had always been aware of it and listened to her elders sing praises of The Precious One. She had unconsciously come to worship him. She wasn't the only one to revere him. Many villagers loved this man in a high position but with more than a hint of humanity in him. His death was a common thing in eastern Tibet.

Delicious fried bread

The Living Buddha's worshippers made him sit in a sitting position, his hands extended in front, and his fingers curled. They then covered the body with crude rock salt. It took two large salt sacks and was very effective at embalming Living Buddha. They painted his face with gold and placed him in an elaborate container where he sat before them all as an idol.

Drolma had even worshiped at his shrine. Drolma's entire religious life was actually centered around this man, which is difficult for Westerners to grasp. It was not a barrier to her worship that the man was believed to still be alive through reincarnation in an eight-year-old boy at the same monastery. The incongruity of this situation did not bother the ardent villager. Drolma, as she was contemplating the Precious One's existence, noticed that her eyes drifted further down the wall below her scarf. On a piece of faded pink paper were printed Tibetan characters. It had also been brought into her home before she was even born. Her mother claimed that a Westerner had arrived in the village 12 years ago at dusk. These little bits of printed paper were in his saddlebags, which he was riding on a mule. Her parents felt sorry for him, as he was so tired and dusty, and they invited him to join them for tea. They were amazed to discover that the traveller, with his fair hair and blue eyes, could speak their language. He appeared to be a kind, peaceful person. His home in Guide was known as the Good News Hall. He was about to go to the villages to share the Good News with them. Drolma was at that time afflicted by an eye infection and was impressed when the visitor gave her immediate relief. Two white tablets provided relief for her husband's headache within a short time. He invited the traveller to spend the night with him. After the evening meal, a large number of villagers came to visit. The traveller seemed to feel lighter and his eyes brightened as he explained the Good News to them. They listened and agreed that the Good News was good but could not understand much. The stranger took the leaflets from his saddlebag and explained the meaning to those who couldn't read.

Three villagers worship at the temple.

Drolma's mother was convinced that Drolma and his message were positive, so she stuck the leaflet on the wall, believing that it would do no harm. One never knows! The traveller left early the next morning. He was asked by his mother to stay for a while. However, he said, rather sadly, that there were many villages to visit, and he was their only source of the Good News.

His rather regrettable remark would recur over the years. If this message was as important as he claimed, then why weren't more people going around spreading it in Tibetan villages? She said, with a smug smile, "Why not look at all the priests in our religion!" She thought, "Surely this other religion cannot be very important." But, she was proud of herself and said, "Why, look at all the priests we have in our religion!" Twelve long years

At the temple

An d tonight Drolma looked at the Gospel tract and scarf on the wall and thought about her mother's words.

The Living Buddha, who was dead; and the Saviour, who was alive.

Monks prepare a burnt offering from juniper, 'tsampa'

<u>One of many Living Buddhas</u>

CHAPTER III - THE RAID ON THE MONASTERY

The Precious One was not only revered by the local villagers. T His fame was spreading far and wide. The fame spread so far that even people from distant villages wanted to purchase the valuable possession. They would all have good fortune if the Precious One lived in their midst!

Drolma, who had been sleeping with her family for several hours, was shocked when a gunshot rang out. It broke the stillness of the night. The family was immediately awakened as they had been actively involved in tribal warfare for many years. Night attacks between different enemies were a common occurrence over the years. Sometimes it was about stealing grain or stealing an animal, other times it was about stealing a bride. Whatever the case, it was tense moments of gunshots and hatred that erupted in the darkness. Drolma's brother and father jumped into their clothes and grabbed their loaded rifles from a wall. Strangely, the attack, whatever it was at the time, appeared to have been directed towards the monastery. The village's

fierce watchdog dogs were barking in fury. As they raced up the hill, men and women shouted and fell over each other in the darkness. Drolma's father, following his son, ran out of his gate and a neighbor ran past him, shouting, "Ouy!" They're LuTsung swine! They'll be dealt with!"

The marauders were faster than the villagers, and they fled into the night before any resistance could be made. The invaders clearly had horses and were quickly away, firing only a few shots, as if laughing at their defenders.

A terrible commotion was heard in the monastery courtyard. The villagers were shocked when the truth became clear. The Precious One was stolen! The enormity of the offense began to dawn slowly on the assembled crowd. The former raiders began to be rebuked with ferocious mutterings. Some villages were there to pursue and punish, but wiser counsel prevailed and the crowd listened as an old priest explained what had happened.

Ashen with sunken cheeks and a pale face, he appeared more like a corpse as he stepped into the moonlight from the shadow of the veranda. He stumbled nervously with his rosary and addressed the crowd. He said that the thieves had made a hole in the wall's exterior using the traditional method. They must have each attached a piece of sharp metal to one of their boots and dug away silently for a while. Three to four men were able to pass through the hole once it was large enough for one man. One of them had blown the poisonous fumes of a drug into several priests asleep nearby, thus ensuring that the monastery was not alerted. One of the watchdogs had been muffled by another, and a third ran to the main gate to open it from the inside to allow the thirty to forty intruders. They were all heavily armed with knives and rifles, and had their horses tethered to them.

It was all done in a flash! The monastery dog was unable to escape and was immediately shot. This was the first shot that alerted the village about a visitation. The advance party had already made their way to the inner court and forced their way through the padlocked doors. They had seized the Precious One with uncanny haste. The old priest's voice suddenly became a sob.

"You all know the rest. "The Precious, the Precious...They have been too smart for us." He or his listeners did not realize that the idol would be kept so tightly that it could never be returned to its legal place. They would also have to make a long pilgrimage to pay homage to it in its new home. To construct a highly elaborate container for the idol, the new owners called a carpenter from Guide. A pane of glass was even brought all the way from Xining to cover the front. Although the insult they received that night was something that could only be healed by time, the angry people only had one thought: revenge. They were more embarrassed by the fact that they could not attack a tribe so much stronger than them. Conscription had sadly decimated their village, which was located near the Chinese frontier.

The moon became cloudy and thunderous sounds reverberated throughout the sky. It dispersed the crowd. The first heavy rains began to fall before most of the people could reach their homes.

Drolma was very nervous during the long absence of her father. Drolma was initially very nervous.

She quickly took out her tiny prayer-wheel and began to turn it. She found something to do, but it did not bring her peace of mind. Her mother was looking straight at the monastery from the top of the ladder, having climbed the wooden ladder. After the shooting stopped and she could hear the voices of the returning villagers, her mother climbed down the ladder, calling to her daughter, Drolma, "Get the fire started, Drolma!" Even though her fingers were more awkward than usual, the little girl was happy to help. Her mother opened the front door to find a hammering sound. To confirm that it was her husband, she called out loudly and removed the heavy planks which were wedged between the doors. Then, her mother opened the door to admit her men and loosen the chain latch.

They all crossed the courtyard to the main room, where the teapot was singing and blazing a fire. The men were not cheered by even this sight. Both were in a rage. Drolma was furious at his father's insult to the village. Yes, his grandfather and father, as well as his great-grandfather, had lived in the village their entire lives. But, never before had there been an such an affair like tonight. He had a lot of tribal stories in his mind, which were passed down from father to child. He was determined to exact vengeance on the thieves. The mother finally persuaded them all to have some hot tea and they began to tell the women about what had happened in the monastery.

Drolma and her mom were shocked by the news. The Precious One has gone! The precious one was gone.
"Gone, gone! She's gone!" she softly moaned to herself and her eyes fell silently.

Village View

P reparing tea

CHAPTER IV - THE MYSTERY DANCE
OF ALL TIBET

Drolma was just fifteen years old when the monastery officials decided that they would revive a gala day that hadn't been celebrated in many years. It was announced widely that a grand festival would take place on the monastery grounds on the nineteenth of the fourth month. Horsemen were sent to notify nearby villages. There was great anticipation among the women of the community?

This celebration's origin was fascinating and well-known to even small children. A certain ruler had razed all monasteries in the border area between China and Tibet long, long ago. Some claimed he was a Chinese ruler while others believed he was Tibetan. His race, however, was not important. He didn't know that his savage act would be remembered hundreds of years later in many monasteries and hamlets long since rebuilt. Some of the priests performed the Mystery Dance of Tibet to commemorate his punishment.

Drolma, her mother-in-law and sister-in law pulled out their finest gowns from the wooden box that had been stored for many months. Two older women made their elaborate trimmings, which would be hung right down from their backs above the fine plaits. These were narrow strips of different colours of cloth, on which were sewn large convex silver ornaments that were as large as a saucer. These ornaments were made of beaten or engraved sterling silver and were decorated with polished wood and stones. Drolma was not married so she had to be content with her jangling coins of copper. She often longed to see the beautiful trimmings of her elders. After all the heavy earrings, bracelets, and silver rings had been polished, the family went to bed. Drolma was very excited and couldn't wait to get up in the morning.

The household set out to climb the hill to the monastery as soon as it became light. Drolma was soon joined by several other girls her age. They held hands and remained together for most of the day, apparently to draw courage from each other. They were able to have several flirtations with other young men who were similarly affected. The girls ran away helter-skelter with giggles whenever daring males approached their ears.

These outings offered great opportunities for business. That was at least the view of the itinerant peddlers, who arrived early to set up their stalls. Around noon, several hundred people were gathered. Some of the early arrivals were now hungry and sat on the hillsides, eating bread and sipping tea that had been brewed on an outdoor fire. A few people had bought a copper coin at one of the stalls, and they were enjoying a boiled potato. The dance began and everyone was happy. A few people had walked down to the shaded groves, where they found a small wooden structure built over a stream. A large prayer cylinder was kept in this building, which was powered by running water. This was the site of a pilgrimage by a Tibetan nun, a shaved head and a devout Tibetan nun.

Two tiny monks blow white conch shells.

Slowly, the curtain was raised and the priests began to stream out under the direction of the chief steward for the monastary.

Many of them held large drums with long handles that resembled baby rattles.

A conch shell blowing and horn blowing began. Two priests were seen on top of the main monastery buildings in their red robes, and high-quality wool hats. The roosters' combs were reminiscent of the tails on the backs of these high-crowned hats. Two priests were blowing eight-foot long copper horns that sounded like telescopes. The sound was small and weak, but it was not dissimilar to the amount of effort required to produce it.

Two little acolytes from the monastery began simultaneously to blow white conch shells. It was an equally boring sound. The holiday crowds heard the call and began to pour back into the monastery grounds.

The main courtyard was where the dance was to take place. A tall prayer flag pole, with its fluttering cloth prayers flags, reached high up from the center of the court. Many of the villager climbed the stone staircase from the Prayer Hall up to the main court. The majority of the villagers walked up to the flat roof and took seats that allowed them to look down on the open space below. Drolma and her friends were among them. The group made a beautiful picture in the sun, their scarlet kerchiefs tucked on their heads at an unorthodox angle. Their bright cheeks, shining white teeth, and infectious laughter made many older people envy their youth. One of the girls accidentally let her boot protrude past the roof's edge. A guard in the court below gave a loud smack to the boot with his long stick immediately. It is important to preserve the monastic etiquette!

The priests were chanting in Prayer Hall all this time. Their monotonous voices ended abruptly with the sound of brass cymbals, blasts of horns, and beating drums. Slowly, the door curtain was raised and the priests streamed forward under the commanding gaze of the chief steward for the monastery. A dozen or more priests climbed into the high-heeled boots that had been left outside and took up the front seats on one side of the roof. They formed the orchestra! All of them sat cross-legged, on a ready-made rug. Many of them held large drums with long handles that looked more like baby rattles. They beat these drums in quick, jerky movements using a long, curved stick. Some of the other members of the orchestra used heavy cymbals to clash with one another, while others had long resonant trumpets. As the priests' constant chanting ranged from rallentando and allegro without warning, the effect was anything but musical.

The courtyard was lively and vibrant as the sun shined brightly. The gala day was enriched by the scarlet and blue dresses, deep red cloth robes worn by some men, flashing silver ornaments and stamping of rough leather boots when late-comers arrived. There was also the cry of a child who was being crushed by the crowd. Drolma was so enthralled by the events around her that she didn't even notice a flock of white and blue jays flying overhead. Her second brother, who was also a birder, came over to chat for a while. After taking his final vows to the priesthood, he was quite a man.

Within a few minutes, he shared with Drolma some shocking news. One of the young priests was found reading a book on the Western religion. It was called John's Gospel. Drolma's brother was told by Drolma that it was a true story about a Living Savior who once died for the sins in the world. It was

given to the young priest by Drolma's brother when he visited one of the border villages last year. Drolma's brother had once told him that if the book was true, the monastery would be in trouble and he was going away. The senior priests knew about this and ordered the lictors to punish the young priest. He was not permitted to attend the dancing today.

The brother whispered, "But the beating won't change him." He added, a little awkwardly, "He's changed somehow." Drolma thought suddenly of the pink leaflet that was hanging on the wall at her home, and the man who brought it. However, the occasion did not allow for deep thought. So many amazing things happened!

Two small, seven-year-old acolytes dressed up as devils and bounced down the stone steps. The crowd was amused when they started to use the batons to order the people who were too close to the centre court. It was warming up now!

The chief steward, with his long gilded blade, stepped forward and took a prominent position at the top of the stairs. Now the celebrations began in earnest. A few priests emerged from behind the Prayer Hall Curtain, carrying on a frame an effigy representing a man nearly three feet tall. One of the priests performed a series of rites that ended with water being flicked in all directions. The frame was moved to the side and dance began. A tall priest appeared first, completely hidden under a stunning and intricately embroidered gown made of stiff kingfisher blue satin. He was wearing an enormous imitation ox head, which made him seem a foot taller than normal. The second ox was next. They were accompanied by an orchestra as they descended into the courtyard. The two dancers began to circle the pole. They danced slowly, with measured steps and their arms extended outstretched. Finally they ran up the steps behind the curtain. The group was followed by about 12 other masqueraders, each wearing elaborate satin costumes and all dressed in exquisitely designed gowns. One dancer wore the head of an vulture and several others. One of the dancers was carrying a large sword, and he held in his left hand a bowl made out of a human skull. They were all the guardians of religion, who kept Lamaism alive despite all its enemies.

After they had danced in pairs, the performers moved in slow-moving circles together. Many elderly, devout women ran forward and bowed in obeisance to the performers as they finished their dance.

Drolma didn't fully grasp the symbolism of the dance but was fascinated by the flashing swords, colourful dresses and other ritualistic elements. The two children, disguised as devils, stumbled down the steps with great skill and a very creative movement after the adults had left the stage. The two little acolytes, disguised as devils, jumped high into the air while simultaneously revolving to land on the other side. This act of miniature performers was a hit with the crowd. The Chief Steward gave the little boys a low command and they continued on for quite some time. They were cheered at the end.

A large flat tray was brought down the steps and laid on the ground in front the pole during the pause that followed the end. The contents of the tray were clearly visible to the spectators, including the man made from tsamba (roasted and ground barley). It looked very real. Like the one on the frame this figure was supposed to be the villain of the piece. He was the ruler who had decimated the monasteries so many years before!

The ox continued dancing and finished the move by kneeling in front of the tray and slashing at his target with his sword. The image was hacked to pieces by other dancers, who followed his lead with much zeal. When one of the dancers took out a long woollen cord that represented the victim's intestines, the final crescendo occurred. He waved it exultantly at the tip of his sword and tossed it high into the air. One of the little devil boys grabbed it eagerly as it fell. The rest of the corpus was thrown around in a similar fashion and then carefully picked up. This great enemy of monasteries was the target of vengeance!

The orchestra led the dancers and priests, who performed loudly as a finale to this childish but devilish performance. They then walked out in one file. Everyone followed the procession to witness the final act, with the effigy at the front. The priests set up a fire in the courtyard and cast the effigy as well as the collected pieces of the 'corpse' into it. This was to the

accompaniment of intense chanting and an inexplicable clamour coming from the orchestra. This was a celebration that reminded me of Guy Fawkes's!

After the dance had lasted several hours, it was now getting into the afternoon when the villagers began to disperse. Some men from distant villages were already sitting in the shade of trees by the monastery, passing wine bottles from one another. They would only get drunk enough to stagger to the horses and attempt to gallop home safely.

Drolma and her relatives said goodbye to their friends, and returned home to make the evening meal and talk about the day's events. Drolma couldn't sleep at night, so she stayed up all night. She was constantly recalling the words of her second brother and wondering what happened to the young priest who had been beat. The young man was only a few years older than her brother. He was from Guide, a small village just a short distance away. His younger brother, who was about 18 years old, had visited the priest a few months before. Her brother brought the two young men with him to the home. Drolma, who was seated in a dark corner of the room, thought about how handsome and strong her brother. She fell asleep, dreaming of blue silk scarves, ox heads and little devil boys mocking a young priest who was reading about a Savior.

A priest lit a blazing fire.

These figures are considered guardians of religion and have kept Tibetan Buddhism alive to this day.

CHAPTER V - A WEDDING AND A JOURNEY

Drolma knew that the visit by the young man wasn't entirely unexpected.

L was a lucky chance. L by chance. Her parents knew of his friends from the village. After Drolma's visit, her parents carefully broached the topic of matrimony. In a growingly modest manner, she lowered her head and stated that she was very happy to accept it. Next was to contact the priest. He was open to the idea of paying a few dollars to cast the horoscope in favor of the marriage, and he also suggested a suitable day for the ceremony. The engagement was announced by the young man's widowed mom.

Six months later, the wedding was celebrated with lots of feasting and lively banter. Finally, Drolma was able to exchange her copper coins for silver ornaments. The agreement had been made that the couple would stay in their respective homes and only make occasional visits to each other until the birth of their first child. Drolma carried water, helped weed the wheat in the fifth and sixth months, and milked the cows every day. Drolma also continued to reap and thresh in the eighth and ninth months.

It was still dark outside, and it was still very eerie. She would sometimes climb up onto the roof to have a final look at everything. She looked up at the monastery, whose white walls still caught the last rays from the sun. She was curious to see where her brother-in law, the young priest, had gone. There had been so much noise when he disappeared. According to the old priest, he had moved to another monastery for further study. Her brother claimed that he ran away to find a place where the Living Saviour could be taught. The disgrace was felt very strongly by her husband's family. An angry priest had visited her home to look for the missing priest, and they even pretended it was some trivial thing. They had stared at the pink leaflet hanging on the wall, and wanted it to be taken down. Her mother, however, was too superstitious to allow them. Drolma was amazed at her mother's boldness! She had not seen the traveller of far away nor seen his face when he spoke about the One who loves all mankind, Tibetans included.

So it was that two years had passed, and one morning a little boy woke up very early.

Drolma was glad to have a baby boy. The home was filled with joy, and many people were invited to the celebration when the baby was one month old. Drolma was soon taken to his home by her husband with the animals. She felt so sad to leave her childhood home, and she went back around the house for the final time. She would have loved to have taken her Precious One's scarf. But, her mother wouldn't let her. She bowed three times to the scarf, then put her hands together. She then turned her back and began to live her new life.

Five days of riding a mule took her to get to her husband's house. The little group continued to go slowly, despite the beautiful blue skies and bright sunshine. Sometimes the narrow track led through rocky mountain bends and sometimes passed peaceful villages where women and men were busy working in their fields. The tall pole, with its many prayer flags fluttering in the wind, was a common feature of Tibetan homes. They often crossed streams of pebbles that flowed down from the tops of high mountain peaks. They often saw small groups of children playing with their water on the flat ground, where the water was more gentle. As they passed the villages, a few dogs barked and sometimes a particularly fierce one snapped at the mules. They met a Muslim falconer with his large hawk tied to his wrist and sat on his arm in a village they were staying the night. They found out that the man had acquired it young and trained it to hunt small animals. The sharpness of its eyes, which flashed from point to point, seemed to be able to see everything that was going on.

A youg Tibetan family

Drolma's husband suddenly exclaimed as they approached a mountain bend. He whipped his gun around ready to fire. A small brown bear was sitting on the track, basking in the sunlight. After looking at the approaching animals with a bewildered look, the bear rose and began to walk down the hill. Drolma's husband was determined to keep this prize safe. Drolma fired straight at the bear and killed him. They were lucky to be close to a village as the bear was very heavy and the mules were already carrying heavy loads. Drolma's husband sold her bear to a villager and only took its shaggy paws. These paws would be a great deal in Guide's Chinese medicine shop. They were highly valued by the Chinese for their medicinal properties. First, he would dry them at home for up to a week.

Although they could have gotten home faster by crossing the grasslands, the little group would have to pass through the territory of a hostile nomad tribe. The Panchen Lama caravan was being robbed by this tribe on its journey from Qinghai, China to Lhasa. Drolma was unarmed, with the exception of one gun.

They met the sorcerer, who was hurriedly proceeding in the opposite direction. His faded, shabby-red robes, long, matted hair, and heavy pack on his back made him look very lonely. His eyes were dark, gloomy and often vacant. For so many years, he had been the Devil's tool that he was completely submissive to him. He was no longer able to control the spirits like when he became a sorcerer.

Many scars from his neck were caused by tubercular glands. They were so mixed with dirt that Drolma and her husband didn't realize how sick he was. He claimed that he had been staying at Guide's Good News Hall for several weeks. He was feeling much better after the Western missionaries gave him medication for his neck. He was a complete stranger to them, and they had been very kind to him. He reported that they had painted pictures on the walls explaining the doctrine of a Living Savior. He was impressed by what he heard and began to speak quickly about it all. Drolma's husband frowned at the mentions of the Good News and hid his lips in thin lines. He refused to take the Gospel tract that the sorcerer offered to him and he urged his horse forward, telling his wife:

"Come along. "We don't want this. Remember my brother and the shame that has befallen us all. Good News," he said bitterly, "What's great about it? I'd love to know."

Satan, raged in hatred at the Light of the World and shut up another proud heart within the dark prison of ignorance and prejudice.

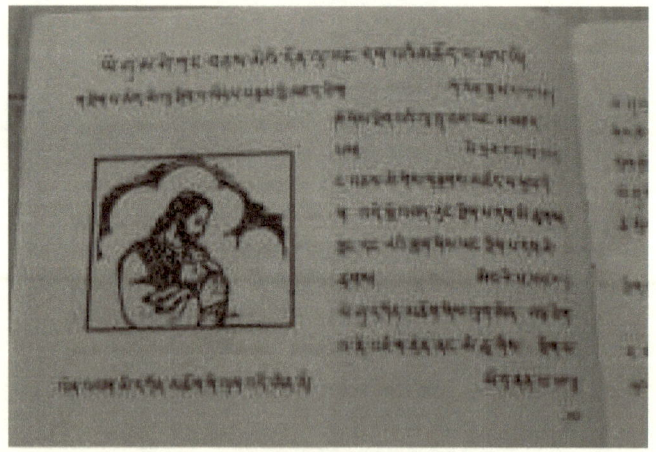

Gospel tracts in Tibetan

<u>Five days was required to travel to the home of her husband.</u>

CHAPTER VI - TWILIGHT IN THE COURTYARD

Rolma was greeted with a warm welcome at her new home. She was not D another one to help with the harvest and housekeeping. The little grandson was taken out of his mother's dress and put into his grandmother's. He was pampered and cared for in the same way as other family members around the globe. Her mother-in law became fond of her new daughter-inlaw because she had a calm disposition and a strong physique.

Mother-in-law, a Buddhist devout, had several shrines around the house. The evil spirits were also offered a bowl full of flour every morning and evening by her. She hoped that this would placate them and keep their misfortune away from their household. She was embarrassed by the stigma associated with her son's repentance and disappearance from the monastery. The long, expensive trip she made to see a Living Buddha in a faraway place to repent her son's sin had been a shameful experience for her. Her mother still longed to find him. He had been her light for over twenty years but now she couldn't help but think of him with bitterness.

Guide is a small, walled town on the banks the Yellow River. These occasions were when they purchased cloth, sugar, or a household utensil or a little bit of sugar. Drolma's husband often took donkey loads wood for the Guide streets in the off-season. The famous fair was held in a beautiful park two miles from Guide on the "double sixth", the sixth day of the sixth lunar month. The fair was a success because all the border races would be there. All the border races, including Muslims, Chinese, Tibetans and tribespeople who had intermarried, were expected to be there.

Dr. Olma received a warm welcome at her new home.

RaGun's little family decided to attend the fair. They went down to Guide on the 5th in their finest clothes and ornaments. They stayed in an inn at the west suburb. While the inner courtyard was full of holidaymakers and tourists, the large outside yard was filled with the sound of several hundred yak tied there. These yak were part a caravan of nomads that had traveled over 100 miles from Rajar. They would soon be back, having exchanged their woolen for flour sacks in a matter of days. The nomads who didn't want to live in the cramped inn rooms had pitched their tent in a corner in the yard, amongst the yak. They would then sleep peacefully in the sheepskins they had made, surrounded only by the snorting and munching beasts.

Drolma's mother was a Buddhist devout. This picture shows a woman turning a large prayer rod.

Drolma was accompanied by her son, and her mother-in law, as she set out to walk in the dark. They had to pass by the tent of the nomads before they could leave the front gate. They noticed a small crowd at the tent's mouth as they went. The men gathered around a brightly colored picture and listened intently to the speech. The yaks began to enter the yard. It was then that the women had to stop at the tent's mouth until the animals left. The voice said:

"S o, the son ran away from home to a faraway place." Drolma looked at her mother-in law as she started looking at her. This person was who?

they were expressing their grief? The voice kept telling of the son's sin conviction, repentance and return to his father's home. Drolma's mother in-law realized that these incredible words had nothing to do her son. The speaker continued to speak of a Heavenly Father waiting to welcome any sons who would only return home.

Two women stood forward in an effort to see the speaker and were surprised to find a Westerner, someone who could speak the language like them. Drolma's mother in law recognized him instantly.

This man and his family had traveled up to RaGun many years ago with their young daughter. They wanted to rent rooms in the village and spend a few months there. They stated that they wanted to share the Good News with everyone. They had warned the village against the new religion and had caused the necessary antagonism. No one would rent rooms. One of the men suddenly had an idea. After several quick consultations with others, the man told the missionaries that there was a courtyard with rooms for rent on the outskirts the village. It was so spacious that the missionary went to inspect it. The missionary could immediately occupy the space, with his family as the only tenants. He was happy to learn that they wouldn't have to share the

courtyard or be cramped with other families. The rent was paid and the family moved into their new home. The villagers went home to have a good time and laugh. All the previous residents of the compound had died from leprosy and would never again be inhabited. The villagers rented the property to missionaries in the hope that their children and grandchildren would contract leprosy. This would end the threat to the Good News religion.

If the villagers knew what the missionaries knew, the hilarity would have subsided. His Master sent him and his as lambs amongst wolves and He promised that "Nothing shall ever hurt you." Drolma however knew nothing about all this and she couldn't look away from the man's eyes tonight. It was such peace! It was not known that the missionary had been absent from her family for several months due to internal strife. He had not received any letters of welcome from his parents, who were both elderly, nor many friends over the oceans. He was totally cut off from the help and advice of his headquarters. She had no idea about the small graves that were nearby.

Sh e didn't know that his peace was something the world could not give him. Poor Drolma was unaware that, even though her ears were hearing a lot, her heart didn't know anything about the Prince of Peace.

People on pilgrimage

Nomad caravan

CHAPTER VII - THE FAIR OF THE "DOUBLE SIXTH"

The sixth morning was a busy day for the townpeople and tourists. Chinese food-vendors carried a pole over their right shoulder and jogged, swinging their foodtuffs from one end of the pole. The traders sold their goods. Everyone raced to the park. After all, who knew that the best stands were not for the first ones? Some of the "early birds" found out that others were there even before they did. They were marking out their places and preventing intruders from getting there until the true tenants arrived.

Many hundreds of Tibetans had already gathered in many different areas by mid-morning on a hot, sunny day. As the men and women moved about in a jumble of bright colours, the green grass became a mass of vibrant colors.

On one side of the fairground were dozens of horses tied together, waving their long tails at the insects. The horses endured the hot day until their owners decided to leave. There were pieces of cloth spread all over the grass, some smaller than a yard square and some larger. These were covered with apricots and raisins, as well as other food, to tempt the Tibetans into parting with their silver dollars. Many of the sellers were Chinese or Muslim and sat under umbrella-shaped, also made from coarse cloth, awnings.

The crowd was gathered in one corner and stood around several feet deep to make a square enclosure. A gallant Tibetan man was inside, and a colorful Tibetan girl sang antiphonally. He sang her a sentence, and then she responded with great mock modesty. The crowd was very appreciative and began to laugh. A Tibetan of great wealth and authority gave scarves to young women who sang best in a tent beneath the trees. These long silk scarves were tied to the girls' sashes. The red, green and yellows flittered in the wind and mixed with the general brightness. They were to entertain the great man at night as a reward for their attention.

<u>Tibetans are drawn from many districts</u>

There were many groups of youths and men gathering under the trees to drink wine, some even before noon. The Cross messengers arrived early to share the Gospel with all who would listen. But as the proceedings became more chaotic and more like Vanity Fair they left. They wondered how they could accomplish their mission of preaching the gospel to every creature. These were Tibetans from far-flung districts that were too many to reach over years. But how could they best be reached in one day when so many were drunk and out for a good time?

Drolma and her group arrived shortly after the missionaries left. She was not happy with the baby and they only stayed for an hour. He had given a few twitches to his face that morning and didn't seem to want to eat. He had more twitches by afternoon and was having convulsions in the evening. The entire family was upset. The husband ran to a Chinese medicine shop, and returned with several costly concoctions. The baby became very ill in the morning. Drolma's husband went into a nearby monastery to ask the priest to perform a horoscope [4].

The priest listened to all the details and advised them to immediately go to the Lord of Sandalwood Idol House. This temple was located in Guide, which is the opposite direction to the fair. It was completely controlled by temple women and is well-known for its miraculous healing properties. It was a place where sick priests and laymen traveled for many days to seek out the cures.

Drolma's husband was somewhat encouraged and ran back to the inn to tell the other about the results of his visit. They immediately took the baby with them and began walking the mile or so to the temple.

CHAPTER VIII - THE LORD OF THE SANDALWOOD TEMPLE

The first sighting of the temple was quite striking. They walked through the ripening wheat fields, wading through a rapid and deep stream, and then ascended a small hill. Through the trees, they could see a

A shining, gilded dome topped a jade green building. Three adults carried the baby, each carrying it in turn.

They sped up to get to the main entrance by climbing a steep incline. They passed through the large gateway and were confronted by two huge, cross-legged idols. A grey-haired temple woman, with her hair in a single, stifling plait, came forward to greet them. She also inquired about the sick one. They were led up a sunny courtyard and given a room close to the temple entrance. Drolma spotted a priest with a pale face hanging meat strips to dry on a string as they passed through the rooms. Evidently, he was a long-term visitor.

Many people lived at the temple as 'patients'. The Abbess gave silver dollars to all of them, and they were instructed on what they should do for healing. Drolma was married to a man who had to go around the temple, turning all the large prayer cylinders. These were located on either side the main entrance. Each was approximately three feet tall and 18 inches wide. After he had turned them all around, he clapped a large iron bell that hung above. This was repeated several times. A huge prayer cylinder was found in a single house. The multicolored, varnished, brightly lit cylinder looked almost like polished enamel. The rope that turned the enormous cylinder, with its many prayers written on it, could be pulled for a fee. Drolma's husband paid nothing if his son could be healed. He quickly turned the cylinder and repeated his prayers.

Drolma herself was to prostrate several hundred times before the main idol shrine. She went into the dimly lighted building where a few old, old women of the temple sat, turning long-handled, fancy, copper prayer wheels.

Drolma, still experienced the same awful shrinking and fear whenever she came near these places. She stood for a moment looking down at the deeply grooved floorboards where hundreds of prostraters had lain. Even deep grooves showing the foot and toe marks were clearly visible. Then taking two pieces of thick felt, to place beneath her hands, she started the wearisome prostrations.

Only deep love for her child impelled her to do this exhausting exercise. Putting her foot in the small grooves, she first fell on her knees, and then with her hands on the felt pads, she shot forward in the longer polished grooves with her face downwards. These movements were all performed so rapidly so as to appear to be one movement. Then she arose upright and repeated the performance. It was customary to do one hundred and eight prostrations without a pause, and Drolma was soon perspiring freely with the unaccustomed and strenuous exercise.

And all the while, the grandmother sat and crooned to the very ill little baby. Presently she decided to carry him around the temple to visit all the idols. Passing the father devoutly at his task and the prostrating Drolma, she went into the inner sanctuary. Before images of three of the Buddhas devotees had placed offerings of the finest of the season's grain. One large butter-lamp, which burned continually, must have contained at least fifty pounds of butter.

From the begrimed ceiling hung various lengthy scrolls and decorative pieces. The whole air was fusty and oppressive, and only after becoming accustomed to the very dim light could the grandmother discern many more fearsome idols in the shadows. Darkness was everywhere, and she felt a choking sensation. Just then, the baby gave a little cry, and she took the opportunity to hurry out into the fresh air once again.

On the main steps were many sick people looking pleadingly towards the shrine, or towards the priestesses who were growing rich on the gifts of the pilgrims. Some of these were too ill to sit up and just lay listlessly waiting for a miracle, which would never happen. Drolma's mother-in-law went around the other courtyards of the temple. In some of these unspeakable things happened. Many visiting priests were about, and she walked past them with downcast eyes, for their coarse boldness oppressed her. At one place she passed a whole row of dried human scapulas (shoulder blades) hanging in a row. On these were inscribed many prayers, mainly the *Om mani padme hum*, and the worshiper had only to set all these moving to have prayed the prayers themselves.

Later in the day the family gathered to eat, but they had no appetite for food, for the baby seemed no better. The whole atmosphere of the temple was not reassuring, and Drolma shivered as she sat nursing the baby in the midnight hours. Her heart cried out to the Precious One, but he could give her no comfort. When presently the little light of the baby's life flickered out, she cried as if her heart were broken. They had done so much and spent all those silver dollars, all to no avail! And now, their little son was no more. If only their deaf ears could have heard the tones of the Good Shepherd, 'Suffer the little ones to come unto me!' But, it was Satan's work to keep them closed, and he was doing his work well.

Before it was light, the baby was placed in a little wayside grave, and the sad party prepared to start at daybreak on their homeward way. Drolma paid one last visit to the many-armed idol Chen-re-zig, the patron saint of all Tibet.

Before the idol had been placed a withered cucumber, the pathetic offering of some poor woman who could not afford anything greater.

Drolma with her husband and mother-in-law went on the sorrowful day's journey back to RaGun. Mercifully the curtain was drawn for her on the greater sorrows that were yet to come.

Tibetans resting while on their journey

Tibetans turning the prayer wheels

CHAPTER IX - UNCLEAN! UNCLEAN!

The next few years passed away, largely governed by rotating crops and monastery festivals. At the New Year Season following on the death of the baby, Drolma's mother-in-law was suddenly taken ill with pneumonia. She died after a few days. So the young couple were left to carry on alone. With increasing taxation to pay to the monastery, they were finding life a hard grind. Another little son was born to them, only to die of tetanus in the first week of life. How could it be otherwise when they had never learnt cleanliness in caring for a newborn baby?

But the worst was yet to come. During the years since his marriage, Drolma's husband had often been unwell and listless for no apparent reason. He noticed a series of small lumps growing under the skin of his face and head, some being the size of a pea, some larger. One morning when he awoke, his face was more puffy than usual, and as Drolma looked at her husband, the terrible truth dawned on her. Her husband had the dreaded disease, leprosy! A leper! He himself had feared that it was so, and now, they both knew the disease could no longer be hidden from other eyes. Drolma was horror-stricken, and she went about the daily tasks distraught and numbed. What would they do? Everything seemed to be shattered about them. As lepers were not permitted to remain in Qinghai[5] Province, they both knew that her husband would have to go far away. In addition, ever afterwards, they would be separated.

After dark one night, they crept forth to wend their way up to the monastery not very far away. There a sympathetic priest cast the horoscope for Drolma's husband. He was to do a pilgrimage to several of the sixty monasteries around Guide and Hualong, and gradually wend his way into Gansu Province to Lanzhou, the capital[6]. There he might find refuge and shelter at the leprosy hospital in connection with the Good News Hospital. This was certainly a propitious horoscope, for the leprosy hospital run by the missionaries was the only one in the whole of northwest China. In this place, the Lord's servants are seeking to obey his command to cleanse the lepers, and many proud Muslims and priest-ridden Tibetans within the leprosy hospital walls have found the Saviour.

Spirit house

It was the last place to which Drolma's husband would have chosen to go. But, in his extremity and helplessness, he was at last in the position to learn what was good about the so-called Good News.

T he priest said that the leper had in some way offended the spirits, to have contracted the disease. But it was freely whispered by some in the village that an enemy had put the leprosy germs in some food that had been served after a feud many years ago. Others said that in his childhood he had played with an unsuspected boy leper and so contracted the disease. But the real source of infection was never known, and only after years of the slow out-working of the loathsome disease did all the terrible implications dawn on him. One morning after the roosters had started to crow, and while the stars were still shining in the sky; the outcast pilgrim bade a lingering and tearful farewell to his young wife. Then with his pack on his back and a long staff in his hand, Drolma's husband walked slowly away into the chilly morning – leaving forever the home of his fathers, leaving it with no son to carry on the tradition, and leaving behind an unprotected and uncared for young wife who would be at the mercy of all and sundry.

By this time, Drolma was twenty-two years old and without husband or child. Her own mother had passed away, and she could not face the reproach of going back to live in her father's house. So gradually, the inevitable happened, and she set out to wander from temple to temple. The few remaining acres of her husband's land she placed in the care of a distant cousin of his. This relative was to remit a small sum of pocket money to her husband every year. But, once Drolma was well out of the way, the cousin conveniently forgot his obligations.

The story of her wanderings during the next seemingly endless ten years would be sad reading. Staying for various lengths of time in the different villages connected with each monastery, she earned her food and sometimes clothing by living the sinful and degrading life of a temple woman. One day she learnt from a traveller that her husband had died in the leprosy hospital. This traveller, who was an old villager from RaGun, said it was reported that her husband had "eaten the Western religion" for several years before his death.

Drolma was not especially upset by the news of her husband's death, for to her he had died years before, and her present life was such, as to deaden many of the finer feelings. But she fell to thinking about the Western religion. What power did it possess to make such a man as her husband change round completely and believe in it? He had been *so* opposed to it all. Drolma wished she knew. Underneath all her sin and frequent toneless laughter, she was desperately hopeless and uncomforted. Many times, she had tried to recall what she had heard about the Living Saviour, but it all seemed indistinct and remote from her daily life. And then, her eyes had become badly infected so that she was almost blind.

Spirit house

It was the last place to which Drolma's husband would have chosen to go. But, in his extremity and helplessness, he was at last in the position to learn what was good about the so-called Good News.

T he priest said that the leper had in some way offended the spirits, to have contracted the disease. But it was freely whispered by some in the village that an enemy had put the leprosy germs in some food that had been served after a feud many years ago. Others said that in his childhood he had played with an unsuspected boy leper and so contracted the disease. But the real source of infection was never known, and only after years of the slow out-working of the loathsome disease did all the terrible implications dawn on him. One morning after the roosters had started to crow, and while the stars were still shining in the sky; the outcast pilgrim bade a lingering and tearful farewell to his young wife. Then with his pack on his back and a long staff in his hand, Drolma's husband walked slowly away into the chilly morning – leaving forever the home of his fathers, leaving it with no son to carry on the tradition, and leaving behind an unprotected and uncared for young wife who would be at the mercy of all and sundry.

By this time, Drolma was twenty-two years old and without husband or child. Her own mother had passed away, and she could not face the reproach of going back to live in her father's house. So gradually, the inevitable happened, and she set out to wander from temple to temple. The few remaining acres of her husband's land she placed in the care of a distant cousin of his. This relative was to remit a small sum of pocket money to her husband every year. But, once Drolma was well out of the way, the cousin conveniently forgot his obligations.

The story of her wanderings during the next seemingly endless ten years would be sad reading. Staying for various lengths of time in the different villages connected with each monastery, she earned her food and sometimes clothing by living the sinful and degrading life of a temple woman. One day she learnt from a traveller that her husband had died in the leprosy hospital. This traveller, who was an old villager from RaGun, said it was reported that her husband had "eaten the Western religion" for several years before his death.

Drolma was not especially upset by the news of her husband's death, for to her he had died years before, and her present life was such, as to deaden many of the finer feelings. But she fell to thinking about the Western religion. What power did it possess to make such a man as her husband change round completely and believe in it? He had been *so* opposed to it all. Drolma wished she knew. Underneath all her sin and frequent toneless laughter, she was desperately hopeless and uncomforted. Many times, she had tried to recall what she had heard about the Living Saviour, but it all seemed indistinct and remote from her daily life. And then, her eyes had become badly infected so that she was almost blind.

Temple site where many search for help

CHAPTER X - VAIN REPETITIONS

t is not in the religion of a Tibetan priest to be of any kind of service to his

I fellow men, that is, any kind of loving service with an altruistic motive. He will perform religious rites for his subjects, who are intimidated by him and all he represents; but only for money will he perform these rites. Occasionally one finds a man of more sympathetic nature who is the exception to the rule, but he is so rare as to be non-existent.

The established religion of Lamaistic Tibet is known as the Yellow Sect. With the exception of two monasteries, one at Guide in Qinghai and the other at Labrang in Gansu, all the scores of monasteries in the country bordering on northwest China are monasteries of the Yellow Sect. The rules and vows are strict, but the daily life and practice tends to become irregular. While some monasteries may be truly celibate, some have a reputation for having sunk into infamous sin and immorality.

Drolma knew something of monastery life, and she knew it was futile to try to seek help for her eyes. They were very painful, so she took her belongings and last few coppers and set off to walk the three days to Guide. Maybe she could buy some medicine that would give her relief. As she walked and frequently stumbled along the dusty road, she looked so ragged and forlorn that sometimes a passing traveller took pity on her and gave her a piece of dried bread or a handful of *tsamba*.

On the third day of her journey, she was sitting wearily by the roadside, when a little procession came past. A tall priest was leading a great black horse. On this was seated a tiny boy about four years old. Straining her sore eyes, Drolma saw that the child was wearing a stiff-brimmed, bronzecoloured hat, surmounted by a kind of Maltese Cross. Also, his robes were of elaborate yellow. Immediately she recognized that he was a Living Buddha and prostrated herself until the procession was passed. Then she got up and looked after them. There were several horses and quite a number of muscular, brutal-looking priests guarding the little boy. The child was very tired and quiet and just looked at her with rather pathetic big brown eyes as he passed. Drolma had heard of the search for a new Living Buddha in connection with a monastery a week's journey away, and she supposed this was he. After the death of the old Living Buddha, a temple consultant had told the hierarchy of the monastery that they must conduct their search for the reincarnation in the region to the northeast of Qinghai Lake[7], so after much casting of horoscopes and much intrigue the priests were bringing back the Living
Buddha in triumph. Such is the iniquitous system that ruins the lives of little boys before they are even aware of life. Eventually Drolma arrived on the streets of Guide, and as she wandered aimlessly along, her ears caught the sound of chanting. She looked up to find she was passing a large Chinese temple with an impressive doorway. She followed the many that were entering the temple, and peering with her sore eyes, she noticed many largesized figures of various idols. These were made of paper and highly coloured. One had a book and pen in which he was supposedly writing the good and bad deeds of everyone.

Drolma went up the central path, brightly decorated with many paper flags. There was something very unusual happening, and seeing a small acolyte standing nearby, Drolma asked him what it was all about.

"It is a Day of Prayer for the nation," he replied. "Tibetans, Muslims, Taoists, Buddhists, and Confucianists are all combining here to pray for peace. It is lasting for eight days."

Drolma was amazed and threaded her way to the first little temple. Here the Taoist priests in their grey robes, with their long hair neatly knotted to show through a hole in the top of their hats, were bowing down to the written page and reciting prayers in a low voice. Further, along, the Confucianists were saying prayers. A Tibetan priest and acolytes on their platform were sitting in two long rows facing one another, with cymbals and conch shells. In yet another courtyard the Buddhist priests were chanting at great length in toneless voices. Many laymen were gathered, and numerous parents whose sons were away at war were devoutly bowing down and making their supplications. Some were burning paper for the dead on a little open fire.

The din of pathetic, futile praying was everywhere, and Buddhist rosaries abounded; there was an air of hopelessness everywhere.

Coming out on the streets once again, she asked a Chinese lad where the nearest monastery was. He said it was just outside the city, but her eyes were so badly swollen and inflamed that she could not see clearly and offered the boy five coppers if he would lead her to the monastery. This offer, being accepted, she held out her stick, which he grasped. She took the other end, and slowly they proceeded through the city and beyond to the monastery gate. There the boy scampered off, and she went inside.

CHAPTER XI - THE ULTIMATE TRIUMPH

T he Menyag Monastery was just across the fields from the Good News Hall. Seeing the serious state of Drolma's eyes and her dirty, travelstained appearance, a priest cast the horoscope in favour of her making an immediate visit to the Good News Hall. Many of the priests from this monastery were frequent visitors to the mission station. They were extremely glad to have medical help from time to time.

Two daughters of Tibet

T herefore, towards evening, this Tibetan woman, lonely, suffering, and unloved, stumbled into the courtyard of the mission. The missionaries thought she was an elderly woman with her grey hair and jaded appearance. As they hastened forward to welcome her, they noticed her old green gown with its orange trimmings, her matted hair with its untidy plaits hanging down her back. They were shocked at the state of her eyes and set to work at once to treat them. Realizing that the woman was destitute, they made her comfortable for the night, and having provided a bowl of steaming hot food they committed her to God in prayer and went to bed.

Only that morning the missionary had been reading the twenty-fifth chapter of Matthew, and it had impressed him afresh. In spite of some caustic comments he had heard about 'Rice Christians' uttered by some who thought themselves wise and far-sighted, he still knew that he personally could not shrug his shoulders and have done with the physical needs of his fellows. He prayed often that he might have the spirit and wisdom of his Master. And so his household warmed and fed this still young derelict of life. The missionaries were amazed to learn that Drolma was only thirty-two years old, and their hearts ached when they heard her story. Perhaps the uppermost thought in their mind was, "If only…if only there had been someone to tell her of Christ clearly, years ago, she might have been saved from all this." For over twenty years they had lived, prayed, and preached in Tibetan country, but there were limits to what two people could accomplish. Reinforcements had come from time to time. However, for some the altitude had proved too rigorous, for others living conditions too hard, and for some, the loneliness of isolation more than they could bear. The few, who had persisted, could be numbered on one hand. They had had very little to encourage them, for no Tibetan had yet openly confessed Christ and been baptized. But the seniors continued year after year, "enduring as seeing Him who is invisible."

Drolma stayed many days until her eyes were quite healed. Every evening she had opportunity to hear clearly about the Living Saviour. And, because at last she was aware of her deep need, she drank in the message of hope. The Saviour was becoming increasingly personal to her, and she learnt about the solace of true prayer. On Sundays while some sauntered into the place of worship, Drolma always stopped at the threshold and put her hands together. This act of reverence was all the more impressive because of her ragged appearance. Then she proceeded bare-footed into the chapel and sat silently through a long service in a language that she did not understand (Chinese). Day by day, she was learning to memorize the chorus,

> "I do believe, I do believe,
> That Jesus died for me,
> That on the Cross He shed His blood,
> From sin to set me free." [8]

Although she had plenty of difficulty adhering to the tune, the resulting effort was shear music to the ears of those who taught her! But when the time came to confess Christ openly to the priest at her late monastery, she feared, and not without cause. In her direct common-sense way, she said to the missionary,

"If I become a Christian openly, where will I earn my living? At once they (the priests) will turn me out, and I have to eat!"

The missionary knew that he was facing a major social problem. For years, he had pondered on what would happen to those who dared to believe. He knew that at once they would be turned off their lands, which in many cases belonged to the monastery. Thus, they would be deprived of their means of support. If a number thus believed, how were they to earn their daily bread? So far, he had no solution to the problem. But he knew that there would be no liberty for the people of Tibet until the power of the monasteries was broken. And for this, he prayed without ceasing.

The devil was waging a relentless fight for Drolma. He seemed to keep her mind dull, so that while she had flashes of deep understanding, yet at other times her memory seemed to be very bad. Speaking of the Lord, she said to the missionary one evening, "If I forget His name, will it be all right if I call Him 'Heaven'?"

Can any of us who know Him ever forget the matchless name of Jesus? We have had those who prayed for us and taught us to love that name. But what of the thousands like her in eastern Tibet – and beyond? Day by day the ruthless conflict is waged between Satan with his minions and Christ with His servants.

And does the Lord, seeing the glorious triumphant day coming, call in vain today for reinforcements in the great battle? Today is He looking at you in your place of privilege and wondering that you are not an intercessor?

"Behold! NOW is the accepted time; Behold! NOW is the Day of Salvation."

Amy and Norman with their four older children Linnet, Averil, Alastair, and Gavin. (photo taken in 1945)

BIBLIOGRAPHY

- **The Story of Drolma**, China Inland Mission 1951
- **The Man in the Sheepskin**, China Inland Mission 1952
- **Journey into Malaya**, Good News Publishers, 1965
- **May Roy: Missionary to Kashmir and the Philippines**, 1966
-
-

AFTERWORD

It is a pleasure to take part in republishing Amy McIntosh's books. She has vivid way of writing and it creates a very real and engaging piece. I really hope it touches you in the same way as it did me. It is amazing to read this book from over 60 years ago and still feel the similarities of today. Of course the cities have grown many times, so have the schools and the shops, and communication with mobile phones and internet is very different. Still, in many ways life has not changed, most have still not heard about the hope in Christ Jesus.

Amy McIntosh wanted to advocate for the Tibetans and the need to pray for them and to share the gospel, to show each reader the need for this area in giving the eternal hope. She wanted us all to remember the Tibetans and invite them to our Lord's family. Her purpose was the same as we have in Central Asia Fellowship, to glorify His name and to establish His kingdom among the Tibetans in the Himalayas.

Central Asia Fellowship is a network for the gospel among all Tibetan Buddhist people. We network to encourage, equip and share to make our Lord known among the peoples. We do this by: praying together, sharing our prayer requests and sending information and news; providing resources for knowledge and sharing by distributing, printing and publishing music, videos, posters and books; holding training events to help each other to be better equipped for the task and for ministry.

The church is growing slowly among the Tibetans. But in recent years we can see how God is mobilizing and moving people to make His glory known and heard over the Himalayas, more than ever before.

We encourage you to be part of our community and network too, for His kingdom among the Tibetans. You can contact us at *contact@centralasiapublishing.com* to sign up for news, a resource catalogue or information on how you can be more involved.

Christian
Executive Director

MAPS

Map of Greatter Tibet

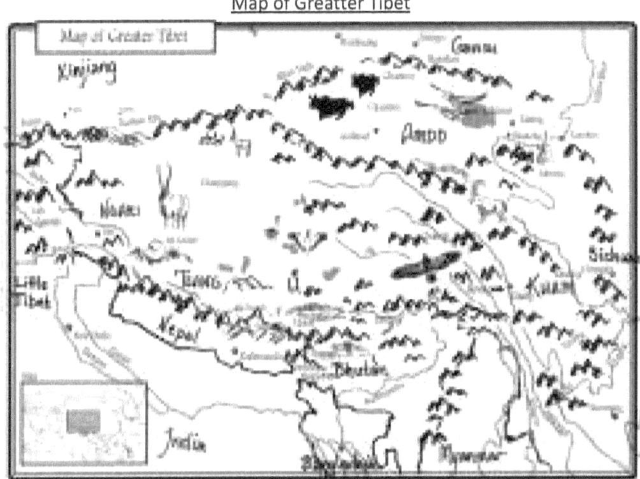

"There are more Tibetans in Chinese territory in the provinces of Qinghai, Gansu and Sichuan than in Tibet proper."

Map of Qinghai

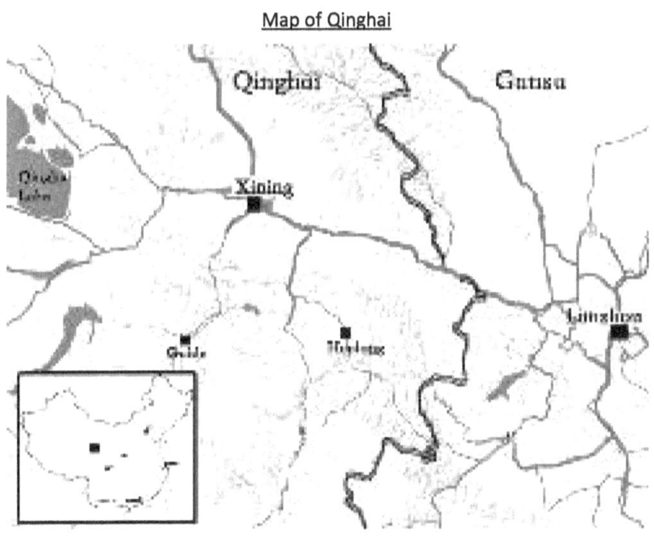

[1] The author used 'lamasery', an old word for Tibetan monastery. (Editor's note)

[2] A chorten (or stupa in Hindi) is an important religious monument in Tibetan areas. Some chortenscontain a relic. (Editor's note)

[3] Original spelling Kweiteh (Editor's note)

[4] "Casting the horoscope".
No Tibetan would dare to take any important (and often unimportant) step in life without finding out from a priest if it were propitious to do so. When a missionary receives a call for medical help, he knows very well that the one who made the request has first consulted the priest for permission. If there is a case of good healing, the credit for this may very well go to the person who cast the horoscope. The ceremony of casting the horoscope is done in a number of different ways (varyingly expensive). One way is for the priest to shake three dice in his hand while chanting a formula. He claps the dice down on the table and by adding up the numbers can announce the decree to his waiting devotee. The whole thing is hocus-pocus and sorcery. Yet, a whole nation is enslaved thereby.

[5] Original spelling Chinghai (Editor's note)

[6] Original spelling Guide and Hwalung (in Qinghai), Kansu province and capital Lanchow (Editor'scomment)

[7] Lake Kokonur, or Kökonur in old from Mongolian meaning blue and clear lake (Editor's note).

[8] 'There is a Fountain' by William Cowper